## VICTORY IN THE PACIFIC

DWIGHT JON ZIMMERMAN,
MILITARY HISTORY CONSULTANT

BY JULIE KLAM

Published by Smart Apple Media, 1980 Lookout Drive, North Mankato, Minnesota 56003

Produced by Byron Preiss Visual Publications, Inc.

Library of Congress Cataloging-in-Publication Data

Klam, Julie.

Victory in the Pacific / by Julie Klam.

v. cm. — (World War II chronicles; bk. 6)

Contents: Japanese conquest at its zenith — The U.S. commanders in the Pacific and Asia — The battle for Guadalcanal —
The battles of New Guinea/New Georgia — The China-Burma-India theater of operations — Attu & Kiska —
The transports of war — Tarawa — Kwajalein — Guam, Saipan & Tinian — Peleliu — Leyte: toehold in the Philippines
— Battle of Leyte Gulf — Liberation of the Philippines — Iwo Jima — Okinawa — Operations Olympic and Coronet:
the planned invasions of Japan — V-J Day — Epilogue: Tokyo war crimes trials and rebuilding of Japan with General
MacArthur as military governor.

ISBN 1-58340-192-X

1. World War, 1939-1945—Campaigns—Pacific Area—Juvenile literature. 2. World War, 1939-1945—Japan—Juvenile literature. [1. World War, 1939-1945—Campaigns—Pacific Area. 2. World War, 1939-1945—Japan.] I. Title.

D767 .K54 2002

940.54'26—dc21      2002017701

First Edition

2 4 6 8 9 7 5 3 1

# CONTENTS:

# INTRODUCTION

World War II was the greatest conflict of the 20th century. Fought on every continent except Antarctica and across every ocean, it was truly a "world war." Like many other wars, over time it evolved. Modern technology and strategic advancements changed the rules of combat forever, allowing for widespread attacks from the air, the ground, and the sea.

For the Chinese, the war began in 1931, when Japan invaded northeastern China. When Germany invaded Poland in 1939, Europeans were dragged into the fray. Americans did not enter World War II until December 7, 1941, when Japan attacked Pearl Harbor, Hawaii.

World War II pitted two sides against each other, the Axis powers and the Allied countries. The main Axis nations were Germany, Japan, and Italy. The Axis powers were led by Chancellor Adolf Hitler, the head of the Nazi Party in Germany; Premier Benito Mussolini, the head of the Fascists in Italy; and Japan's Emperor Hirohito and the military government headed by Prime Minister Hideki Tojo. The Allies included Britain, France, the Soviet Union, China, and the United States. The leaders of the Allies were Britain's Prime

⊬ Benito Mussolini

⊬ Hirohito

Winston Churchill

Minister Winston Churchill, who had replaced Neville Chamberlain in 1940; General Charles de Gaulle of France; the Soviet Union's Marshal Josef Stalin; China's Generalissimo Chiang Kai-shek; and Franklin Delano Roosevelt, the president of the United States. The two sides clashed primarily in the Pacific Ocean and Asia, which Japan sought to control, and in the Atlantic Ocean, Europe, and North Africa, where Germany and Italy were trying to take over.

World War II finally ended in 1945, first in Europe on May 8, with Germany's total capitulation. Then, on September 2, the Japanese signed the document for their unconditional surrender after the United States had dropped two atomic bombs on Japan. World War II left 50 million people dead and millions of others wounded, both physically and mentally.

The war encompassed the feats of extraordinary heroes and the worst villains imaginable, with thrilling triumphs and heartrending tragedies. *Victory in the Pacific* takes readers through the final battles that led to Japan's defeat and the end of the war in the Pacific.

Charles de Gaulle

H Josef Stalin

H Chiang Kai-shek

H (right): Franklin Delano Roosevelt

# Map of German Conquests

- Germany (1939)
- Axis Occupied Territory (1942)
- Italy and Its Territories
- Treaty with Axis
- Allied Powers
- Allied Protectorates
- Neutral Countries
- Vichy France and Territories

FINLAND

NORWAY

SWEDEN

ESTONIA

*North Sea*

*Baltic Sea*

LATVIA

UNION OF
SOVIET SOCIALIST REPUBLICS

IRELAND

UNITED
KINGDOM

DENMARK

LITHUANIA

EAST
PRUSSIA

THE
NETHERLANDS

BELGIUM

GERMANY

POLAND

*Atlantic
Ocean*

LUXEMBOURG

FRANCE

SLOVAKIA

SWITZERLAND

HUNGARY

VICHY
FRANCE

ROMANIA

*Black Sea*

YUGOSLAVIA

PORTUGAL

*Adriatic Sea*

ITALY

BULGARIA

SPAIN

ALBANIA

TURKEY

SPANISH
MOROCCO

GREECE

SYRIA

IRAQ

MOROCCO

*Mediterranean Sea*

PALESTINE

TRANS-
JORDAN

ALGERIA

TUNISIA

EGYPT

SAUDI
ARABIA

LIBYA

# The Pacific Campaign

ALASKA

U.S.S.R.

ALEUTIAN
ISLANDS

**ATTU, KISKA**
*May-Aug. 1943*

MONGOLIA

MANCHURIA

KOREA

JAPAN

CHINA

TIBET

**Doolittle Raid**
*Apr. 18, 1942*

**MIDWAY**
*June 1942*

INDIA

BURMA

HONG
KONG

**OKINAWA**
*April-June 1945*

**IWO JIMA**
*Feb.- March 1945*

**PEARL HARBOR**
*Dec. 7, 1941*

**THE PHILIPPINES**
*Oct. 1944-June 1945*

FRENCH
INDOCHINA

**SAIPAN, GUAM & TINIAN**
*June-Aug. 1944*

THAILAND

BORNEO

DUTCH EAST INDIES

NEW
GUINEA

**TARAWA**
*November 1943*

**U.S. aircraft carrier**

**Battle**

**Allied advance**

**Japanese possession
before Dec. 7, 1941**

**GUADALCANAL**
*Aug. 1942-Feb. 1943*

**Japanese conquest
after Dec. 7, 1941**

**Limit of
Japanese expansion**

AUSTRALIA

# JAPANESE CONQUEST AT ITS ZENITH

From December 7, 1941, to August 7, 1942, the Imperial Japanese army and navy conducted an astonishing campaign of conquest. In just seven months, they captured territory extending approximately 4,000 miles (6,437 km). Japan's borders reached as far north as Attu and Kiska, the Aleutian Islands of Alaska; as far south as the Solomon Islands, just above Australia; as far west as Burma, on the border of India; and, with the Gilbert Islands, almost touched the International Date Line in the central Pacific Ocean.

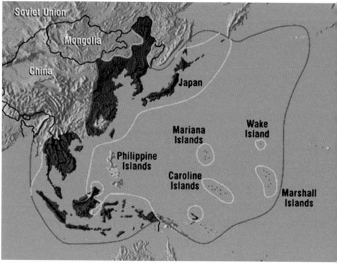

A map of Japan's conquests in the Pacific.

No other country in history had seized so vast a territory in so short a time. That achievement was as frightening as it was breathtaking. If the Japanese war machine could conquer so much so quickly, what possible hope could the Allies have of defeating it?

Three key American victories demonstrated that the Japanese were not invincible: the Doolittle Raid on the Japanese home islands on April 18, 1942; the Battle of the Coral Sea on May 4–8, 1942; and the Battle of Midway on June 4–7, 1942. The Battle of Midway was the most important because it stopped the Japanese advance in the Pacific.

With the Allies' victory at Midway, the initiative passed to the Americans. They would take advantage of it on August 7, 1942, by invading the Japanese-held island of Guadalcanal in the Solomons.

✝ Chester W. Nimitz

### Admiral Chester W. Nimitz

After the Japanese sneak attack on Pearl Harbor, the U.S. Navy in the Pacific got a new commander, Admiral Chester W. Nimitz. With most of its fleet damaged or destroyed and most of its men worried about what would happen next, the U.S. Navy was in need of a great leader to turn things around. Nimitz proved to be that great leader. A bold strategist, Admiral Nimitz knew how to inspire the people under his command. The first example of this was the high-risk Doolittle Raid on the Japanese home islands in April 1942, less than five months after the attack on Pearl Harbor. For the first time ever, U.S. Army Air Force bombers were flown off the flight deck of an aircraft carrier. Many people thought such a thing was impossible. Nimitz was one of the few who didn't. The raid was a success in that it did a great deal to boost U.S. morale.

Nimitz also made brilliant use of the island-hopping strategy, an advance that involved bypassing heavily defended Japanese-held outpost islands and seizing more lightly held ones.

For his excellent leadership, Admiral Nimitz was promoted to admiral of the fleet, a new five-star rank created near the end of World War II.

### General Douglas MacArthur

General Douglas MacArthur was the charismatic, flamboyant, and brilliant son of a Civil War hero. MacArthur was the commander of the

U.S. Army troops in the Pacific during World War II. He was the commander of U.S. troops in the Philippines when a more powerful Japanese force invaded the island nation in December 1941, just after the attack on Pearl Harbor.

Ordered to evacuate to Australia in early 1942 by President Franklin Roosevelt, MacArthur issued a dramatic vow as he departed the Philippines: "I shall return." This became a rallying cry that was fulfilled in late 1944. MacArthur developed and was the first to use the island-hopping strategy. MacArthur was promoted to general of the army, a new five-star rank created late in World War II. He was also one of only two top U.S. leaders in World War II to receive America's highest decoration, the Medal of Honor.

### General Joseph Stilwell

General Stilwell, the top U.S. commander in the combat area named the China-Burma-India (CBI) Theater of Operations, probably had the toughest job of all the military commanders in World War II. Stilwell was expected to fight the Japanese with the fewest men, weapons, and supplies. He also worked under Chinese leader Chiang Kai-shek as commander of the Chinese troops. Stilwell and Chiang Kai-shek did not get

✝ Joseph Stilwell

along. Eventually, Chiang forced him to leave. At the end of the war, Stilwell was one of the commanders of the ground troops for the planned invasion of Japan.

### Admiral William Halsey

Admiral Halsey was one of America's most aggressive and imaginative naval commanders. Early in his career, Halsey saw that naval air power would be important in fighting a war, so he took up flying lessons. In 1935, he qualified as a naval aviator.

Halsey was the naval commander of the Doolittle Raid fleet and many of the successful island-hopping campaigns in the Pacific. Like Nimitz, Halsey was promoted to the rank of admiral of the fleet.

### General Alexander Vandegrift

Marine Corps general Vandegrift led the Marines in the first American invasion offensive in the Pacific: Operation Cactus, the invasion of Guadalcanal, in August 1942. Guadalcanal is the southernmost island in the Solomon Islands chain. The battle to take Guadalcanal from the Japanese was a bitter, hard-fought struggle that lasted for months. But Vandegrift and his Marines defeated the enemy. It was a major victory for the United States.

Vandegrift was the Marine Corps' first four-star general. He was also the first Marine to be awarded both the Navy Cross and the Medal of Honor and to hold the title of general while still in active service.

The Japanese advance in the Pacific had been stopped by America's victory at the Battle of Midway. To begin driving the Japanese back, the United States Marine Corps invaded Guadalcanal, located just 1,200 miles (1,931 km) northeast of Australia.

Guadalcanal was chosen because the Japanese were building an air base on it. With that air base, the Japanese would be able to send bombers to sink supply and troop ships sailing to Australia from the United States. By taking Guadalcanal, the Americans would be able to use the air base against the Japanese and the island as a staging area for later advances against Japan's major base in the region, Rabaul, located on the island of New Britain.

The Marines landed on August 7, 1942. The invasion took the Japanese garrison by surprise. The Marines managed to quickly capture the airfield and establish a defense line inland to protect it. The Marines

✢ American troops invade Guadalcanal in 1942.

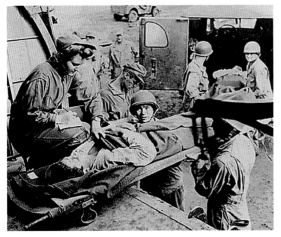

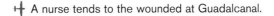
A nurse tends to the wounded at Guadalcanal.

called the airfield Henderson Field, after a Marine pilot who was killed in the Battle of Midway.

It was a good thing the Marines moved inland so quickly. The Japanese quickly sent troop reinforcements. They also regularly sent fleets of warships at night to attack Allied ships and shell Marine positions. Because these attacks were almost as regular as a scheduled train, the Marines came to call them the "Tokyo Express."

The Marines refused to give up, even when the Japanese launched desperate all-or-nothing attacks that would end only when the last Japanese soldier in the attack was killed. These suicidal attacks were called "banzai charges."

It took about six months for the Americans to win the battle for Guadalcanal. While this was happening, General MacArthur was launching his island-hopping advance farther west.

## BANZAI CHARGES

"Banzai" is a Japanese word that means "10,000 years, forever!" Traditionally, it was a cheer shouted in dedication to the life of the emperor. It was also a part of the samurai code of honor that demanded a warrior die rather than accept dishonorable capture. The original samurai were warriors in feudal Japan, roughly like the knights of Europe in the Middle Ages. Samurai practices evolved into a code of conduct in the Japanese military. When it became apparent that the Japanese were about to lose a battle or an island, the surviving troops would assemble and launch a suicidal all-or-nothing attack against the American lines. As they charged, the Japanese would shout, "Banzai!" Thus, the suicidal assaults became known as "banzai charges."

# THE NEW GUINEA CAMPAIGN

The jungle-covered island of New Guinea is located less than 500 miles (805 km) north of Australia. It is the second-largest island in the world. (Greenland is the first.) The Japanese knew that if they could conquer New Guinea, they could hit northern Australia with a powerful air attack or even an invasion. If the Allies could seize control of the island, they could use it as a forward base for the liberation of the Philippines farther north.

By mid-1942, the Japanese controlled the northern half of the island. The Allies, led by General Douglas MacArthur, held the southern half. MacArthur's combined American and Australian troops held the strategically

✠ Australian ground units fight the Japanese in Papua, New Guinea, 1943.

important city of Port Moresby on the southeast tip of the island. The Japanese wanted Port Moresby, for with it they would virtually control the island.

MacArthur knew that the Japanese army on the northern half of New Guinea was too powerful for his troops to attack and defeat. But the islands around the northern coast of New Guinea gave him an idea. For the Japanese, these islands acted as a shield to keep the Allies out. MacArthur saw them as a fence to keep the Japanese in, if he could capture them. MacArthur created a plan to capture key weakly held islands in this "fence." (This was called the island-hopping strategy.) MacArthur kept a strong force at Port Moresby to defend against Japanese attacks. With the rest of his troops, he captured select islands around the north side of New Guinea.

MacArthur's island-hopping strategy not only "fenced in" the Japanese on New Guinea, but it also impressed the U.S. Navy so much that it decided to use the strategy, too, in its advance up the Solomon Islands from Guadalcanal and in the Central Pacific, starting with Tarawa.

# THE CHINA-BURMA-INDIA THEATER OF OPERATIONS

Fighting in the China-Burma-India (CBI) Theater of Operations was difficult for the United States and England. CBI was the most remote combat region. Transport ships carrying troops, weapons, and supplies had to travel halfway around the world to get there. This often took months. Also, CBI was the lowest on the priority list, a distant third after the needs of the forces in Europe and the Pacific.

But CBI was important for two reasons. The first was that the Chinese armies were fighting thousands of Japanese troops in China. The second was that the Allies didn't want to risk having Japanese troops in Burma invading India, just across the Burmese border. If the Japanese did that, China would be totally isolated and forced to surrender.

While the American and British forces fought the Japanese in Burma, they also created two ways to keep Chinese troops supplied. One way was by air, using cargo planes flying from air bases in India to transport supplies to air bases in China. The air route took the cargo planes over the Himalaya Mountains. The pilots flying the route called it "the Hump."

The other way the Allies transported supplies was over a road cut through the thick jungle of northern Burma. This road, almost 500 miles (805 km) long, was called the Ledo Road, after a city on the route. Begun in December 1942, it was not completed until January 1945. It was one of the greatest and most challenging construction projects of the war.

Because of the tremendous efforts made by the Americans and

⊬ Workers with yokes and buckets labor beside a bulldozer on the Ledo Road in the China-Burma-India Theater.

British, China was able to continue the fight against the Japanese throughout the war. This kept thousands of Japanese soldiers from being sent to fight American soldiers and Marines in the Philippines and other Pacific islands.

# ATTU AND KISKA

When the Japanese launched their attack against Midway in June 1942, they also sent an invasion force north to capture Attu and Kiska, the two westernmost islands in the Aleutian Islands chain of Alaska. Though the Japanese were defeated at Midway, they were successful in capturing Attu and Kiska.

Strategically, the islands weren't that important. They were too far north and west to be an effective air base for an attack on America. But politically they were very important. These islands were part of a U.S. territory. And Americans were afraid that if the Japanese weren't kicked off the islands, they'd fight their way closer and threaten the West Coast.

✛ An American Catalina patrol plane searches for enemy activity in the snow-clad mountains of the Aleutian Islands.

Because the region was so remote and undeveloped, it took the Americans almost a year to construct the bases, transport the troops, and build up the supplies needed for the liberation. Finally, on May 11, 1943, the combined U.S. and Canadian liberation force landed on Attu. The defending Japanese garrison fought hard, but in less than a month, it was defeated. Because the fighting on Attu was so hard, a larger invasion force was assembled to liberate Kiska. But when the Allied troops landed on Kiska on August 15, 1943, they discovered that the Japanese garrison had evacuated. The island was deserted!

It took more than a year, but the Allies had reclaimed the American islands.

United States ship- and boatbuilders were asked to construct many types of craft to fight the enemy during World War II. Some of the most amazing were the landing craft constructed by Andrew Higgins and other boatbuilders. These were designed to carry troops, vehicles, and supplies directly to the invasion beaches. Here are just a few of the landing craft that were used throughout the war:

✛ A Higgins boat drops off troops and vehicles during the invasion of Wake Island.

## DUKW

Code-named DUKW (in military language, "D" was for the year of design [1942], "U" meant amphibian, "K" stood for all-wheel drive, and "W" for two rear axles) and called "Duck" by the troops, this transport could travel both over the water and on land. It usually carried 20 well-equipped men. America was the only country that had anything like it.

## LST

Crews of the LST (Landing Ship Tank) said the initials really stood for "Long Slow Target." While the LST would never set any speed records, it made up for its slow pace with its ability to carry a huge amount of cargo. Dozens of tanks or trucks could fit into its hold

 Two LSTs wait in the surf of Leyte Island beach.

(storage space). Most important, unlike other cargo ships that had to dock by a pier and be unloaded by a crane, the flat-bottomed LST could land straight onto a beach and swing open its wide bow doors, and the vehicles inside could just drive out on their own.

## LCVP

The LCVP (Landing Craft Vehicle Personnel) was also called the Higgins boat, after its designer, Andrew Higgins. More than 20,000 Higgins boats were produced, and they carried fighting men ashore everywhere during the war.

In a 1964 interview, General Dwight Eisenhower, who commanded the landing of the troops on D-Day, said that Andrew Higgins's contribution won the war for the Allies. Eisenhower explained:

*If Higgins had not designed and built the LCVPs, we never could have landed over an open beach.*

Tarawa is an atoll in the Central Pacific, part of the Gilbert Islands chain. An atoll is a series of coral islands and reefs roughly shaped into a ring around a lagoon. After Guadalcanal was taken, U.S. Navy strategists decided that they would assault Tarawa and use the new airfield on the islet, Betio, as a forward air base to neutralize nearby Japanese-held island strong points.

Tarawa was the first major trial by fire of America's new amphibious assault plan against a heavily fortified beach. This plan included the first use of the new DUKWs and other landing ships, and the first coordinated use of airplane attacks and naval shelling of the beaches just before the invasion.

The Japanese commander of Tarawa, Admiral Keiji Shibasaki, stated, "A million men cannot take Tarawa in a hundred years." The reason he said this was that Betio was honeycombed with hidden bunkers and other underground shelters that were virtually invisible. From these well-protected sites, Admiral Shibasaki was sure his troops' cannons, machine guns, rifles, and other defenses would destroy any American assault.

U.S. Marines invaded Betio on November 20, 1943. It took the Marines three days to seize the island. But the fighting was the most brutal yet encountered in the war.

Marines wade ashore during the assault on Tarawa.

Tadao Onuki, one of the few Japanese defenders who survived the battle, recalled:

*I kept shooting [my tank's cannon] until the gun barrel became red hot . . . [Yet] under our fire, [the U.S. Marines] came in large numbers, one after another, floating in the shallows, stepping over their friends' bodies.*

The successful invasion of Tarawa proved that an attack could be made against a fortified beach. The amphibious-assault lessons learned at Tarawa would be put to good use in future assaults.

Kwajalein, a Central Pacific atoll in the Marshal Islands, just west of Tarawa, was the next U.S. Navy target after Tarawa. Kwajalein is the largest atoll in the world, and if the Americans could capture it, they would punch a big hole in the island-defense perimeter around Japan.

A number of islands in the Kwajalein atoll were attacked in February 1944. Thanks to the lessons learned at Tarawa, the successful invasion of the Kwajalein islands was completed with fewer casualties than at Tarawa.

The capture of Kwajalein was an important psychological victory for the Americans. Kwajalein was the first piece of Japanese-owned territory to be seized by the United States.

The next stop for the Americans was the liberation of a piece of U.S. territory, the island of Guam.

✛ Flame throwers were used to smoke out the Japanese while soldiers waited patiently for them to come out.

# GUAM, SAIPAN, AND TINIAN

✛ Marines lay low to avoid enemy fire while going to their assigned posts.

Guam, Saipan, and Tinian are part of the Mariana Islands chain, located approximately 1,200 miles (1,931 km) from Tokyo. This island chain was well within the range of the new B-29 Superfortress bombers that the United States wanted to use to attack Japan. There was another reason Americans wanted the Marianas. Guam was a U.S. territory that had been occupied by the Japanese since December 12, 1941, just after the attack on Pearl Harbor.

The Japanese high command expected Admiral Nimitz to send the U.S. Navy and Marines to attack the Marianas, and they were ready.

Operation Forager, the campaign to liberate the Marianas, started in June 1944. Saipan was the first island invaded, followed by Guam and Tinian, both invaded in late July 1944. As before, Japanese troops on the islands fought fiercely against the Americans. In addition, the Japanese navy sailed out in force to destroy the American fleet guarding the landing beaches. The U.S. Navy was looking forward to the fight.

On June 19, 1944, the two biggest naval powers in the world fought the greatest aircraft-carrier battle in history. When it was over, the Americans had decisively won. Officially called the Battle of the Philippine Sea, the confrontation became known as the "Great Marianas Turkey Shoot" because, in addition to a number of major warships sunk, the Japanese lost almost 400 warplanes, compared to only about 130 for the Americans.

By mid-August 1944, Guam, Saipan, and Tinian were solidly in American hands. Soon the Japanese home islands would feel the impact of the bombs dropped by the B-29 Superfortresses.

Peleliu is part of the Palau group of islands in the Caroline Islands chain located less than 800 miles (1,287 km) east of the Philippines in the Central Pacific. The Americans needed to capture Peleliu in order to keep the Japanese from using its airfield to send planes to attack the Philippine island of Leyte, where General MacArthur and his troops were scheduled to land.

The U.S. Marines invaded Peleliu on September 15, 1944. They discovered an island filled with thousands of caves; each one, it seemed, was heavily fortified. As before, the Japanese troops fought with great courage and determination. But the Marines noticed some-

✠ Marines taking a short break while on the island of Peleliu.

thing different about the way the Japanese defenders fought. In the past, at one point during the fighting, usually toward the end, the surviving Japanese garrison would launch a suicidal banzai charge against the American line. This time, the defenders didn't. Instead, they remained in their caves and forced the Americans to come and get them. It took months, and it cost the Americans many casualties. The last Japanese defender didn't surrender until February 1945. But by that time, Peleliu was firmly in American hands. MacArthur's flank, or side, was secure.

# LEYTE: A TOEHOLD IN THE PHILIPPINES

The liberation of the Philippines was the next big objective on the Allied list. With the Philippines freed, Japan would be cut off from the territory rich in natural resources it had seized in the south.

Commanding the invasion force was General Douglas MacArthur, who had been forced to leave the Philippines in the spring of 1942. On October 20, 1944, MacArthur fulfilled the vow he had made back in 1942. Striding onto the beach of the central Philippine island of Leyte, he proudly stated, "I have returned." It was a brave, noble, and possibly even foolhardy thing to do, because the beachhead had not been cleared of enemy troops. Snipers were still hiding in the trees, well within range of the beach. One astonished American soldier who saw MacArthur on the beach gasped, "Hey, there's General MacArthur!" Without turning to look, the soldier beside him said, "Oh, yeah? And I suppose he's got Eleanor Roosevelt along with him."

The battle to liberate the Philippines would last until the end of the war. But by that time, most of the Philippines would be free.

MacArthur arrives in the Philippines during the first landings at Leyte.

# THE BATTLE OF LEYTE GULF

When the Americans landed on Leyte, the Japanese high command knew they had to go all-out in order to destroy the Americans. If they failed in their attempt, they knew defeat would be inevitable. To carry on with the war, Japan needed the vital raw materials of oil, rubber, and various metals in Indochina and the Dutch East Indies. With the Philippines in American hands, Japan would be cut off from those resources.

The Japanese plan to destroy the landing beaches on Leyte and the American fleets guarding them was called Operation Sho-Go (Operation Victory). Three fleets—the Northern Force, the Central Force, and the Southern Force—were assembled and ordered to attack in late October 1944. Operation Sho-Go almost succeeded.

The Northern Force was the only one with aircraft carriers. It was the decoy. It successfully used its aircraft carriers to lure the U.S. Navy Third Fleet under Admiral Halsey, which was rich with powerful aircraft carriers, away from the Philippines. The Southern Force was stopped by the U.S. Seventh Fleet under Admiral Thomas Kinkaid.

But no one spotted the Central Force until it was almost too late. The Central Force under Admiral Takeo Kurita consisted of more than 30 ships, including 5 battleships and 10 heavy cruisers. Two of his battleships, the *Yamato* and the *Musashi*, were the largest ever built. They far outclassed even the most powerful battleships in the American fleet. If this fleet had reached the beachhead and the Americans' defenseless cargo ships, the Japanese would surely have taken Leyte.

The U.S. carrier *Suwanee* sinks after a kamikaze attack in Leyte Gulf, October 26, 1944.

Against this awesome fleet were three small task groups known by their radio call signs—Taffy 1, Taffy 2, and Taffy 3—under the command of Rear Admiral Thomas Sprague. These task groups contained slow, unarmored escort carriers, destroyers, and destroyer escorts. These were some of the smallest warships in the U.S. Navy, and their mission was to support troop landings and attack enemy submarines, not fight enemy surface ships—especially not battleships. But that's what they had to do on the morning of October 25, 1944. And that's what the sailors of the three Taffy task groups did.

It was a David-versus-Goliath type of battle. The Americans were outgunned and outclassed in every way possible. By all rights, it should have been an easy victory for the Japanese fleet. Instead, by their fierce determination and unrelenting efforts, the small American fleet caused the Japanese fleet commander to think he was fighting a huge fleet and would soon be destroyed. He ordered the Central Force to retreat. The landing beaches at Leyte were saved.

# THE LIBERATION OF THE PHILIPPINES

The Philippines is a nation with more than 7,000 islands. One of the largest is the northern island of Luzon, which has the capital city of Manila. The Bataan peninsula is also on Luzon, southwest of Manila. Near the tip of the Bataan peninsula, at the mouth of Manila Bay, is the island of Corregidor. The U.S. troops made their last stand at Bataan and Corregidor before surrendering to the Japanese invaders in spring of 1942.

In early January 1945, General MacArthur's troops worked their way north from Leyte and landed on Luzon. As they liberated the island, they freed the American survivors of Bataan and Corregidor held in prisoner of war (POW) camps. The liberating troops were shocked at what

✠ During the infamous Bataan Death March, May 6, 1942, approximately 10,000 Filipino and American prisoners died.

+ A G.I. carries a girl to safety during the liberation of the Philippines in Manila.

they discovered. The surviving soldiers had been horribly treated, in complete violation of the rules of war. Worse, many had been subjected to the atrocity called the Bataan Death March.

Shortly after their surrender in 1942, American and Filipino troops were forced to march from Bataan to POW camps about 60 miles (97 km) away. The treatment of the soldiers during the march was monstrous. They were given little or no food or water. Anyone who couldn't keep pace with the marchers, for whatever reason, was stabbed or shot to death. Thousands died before reaching the camps. When they arrived, soldiers found the conditions at the POW camps barbaric.

Americans all over were outraged when they discovered what the Japanese had done. They demanded that those responsible be caught and punished. After the war, that demand was fulfilled during the Japanese war crimes trials.

By early 1945, the vast defense ring of fortified islands protecting Japan had greatly shrunk. That ring now consisted of Formosa (Taiwan) and the Ryukyu Islands south of Japan and the Bonin Islands southeast of the home island of Honshu. Okinawa, one of the Ryukus, was the last island on the American invasion list before the attack on Japan itself. But before Okinawa could be taken, the Americans had to seize an island in the Bonins. That island was Iwo Jima.

From the air, Iwo Jima looks like a lumpy pork chop. Its most prominent feature is Mount Suribachi at the southern tip.

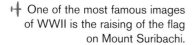 One of the most famous images of WWII is the raising of the flag on Mount Suribachi.

Iwo Jima was located about halfway between Japan and the B-29 air bases on the Mariana Islands. Its location made Iwo Jima strategically important. If America could seize the island, it could use it as an air base for fighter planes that couldn't fly as far as the B-29s. Also, a B-29 that was too damaged to fly back to Guam, Saipan, or Tinian could safely land on Iwo Jima instead of ditching in the ocean.

The Japanese commander on Iwo Jima, General Tadamichi Kuribayashi, did everything he could to turn the island into a death trap for the Americans. He didn't boast about the island's defenses the way Admiral Shibasaki did at Tarawa. He would let the rifles, machine guns, and cannons of his men hidden in their almost invisible and indestructible bunkers and caves speak for him.

The U.S. Marines landed on Iwo Jima on February 19, 1945. From the first moment, the taking of Iwo Jima was one of the bloodiest battles of the war. Out of 30,000 Marines who landed, about 20,000 were wounded and almost 6,000 were killed.

But the taking of Iwo Jima accomplished its mission. Even before the fighting was over, damaged B-29s were landing on the island's airfields. The battle also produced the most memorable photograph of World War II, the flag raising on Mount Suribachi.

# OKINAWA

Okinawa is a 60-mile-long (97 km) island less than 400 miles (644 km) south of Japan. The United States planned to use it as a base of operations for the invasion of Japan. The battle for Okinawa was the last great battle of World War II, and in many ways, it was the hardest.

The Japanese had always been tough fighters. But now, on their last line of defense, they became even more determined. Countless hidden bunkers, like those on Iwo Jima, were created. All the Japanese soldiers and sailors on Okinawa were determined to fight to the last man and kill as many Americans as they could before they fell. In addition, the Japanese commander, Lieutenant General Mitsuru Ushijima, planned to use the native Okinawan militia and even armed Okinawan children against the Americans.

## THE KAMIKAZE

"Kamikaze" is Japanese for "divine wind." The kamikazes were special squadrons of suicide pilots. These men pledged to die for Emperor Hirohito (who was considered divine). And they would do it by deliberately smashing their bomb-laden planes into American warships. During the battle for Okinawa, the kamikazes sunk 36 ships and damaged hundreds more. But not even this terrible and desperate weapon was enough to save Japan from defeat.

But the most frightening weapon in the Japanese arsenal was the kamikaze. The kamikazes were first used in 1944 in the Philippines. But it was at Okinawa that they would be used in full force.

The Americans invaded Okinawa on April 1, 1945. The force included 180,000 troops and about 1,300 warships of all

The USS *Franklin* falls under attack during the invasion of Okinawa.

On April 12, 1945, while having his portrait painted, President Franklin Roosevelt suffered a cerebral hemorrhage and died. He was succeeded by his vice president, Harry S Truman.

When he was vice president, Truman rarely saw Roosevelt. In fact, he was unaware of all the major secrets concerning the war. For instance, Truman did not learn about the top-secret development of the atomic bomb until after he became president. When he was sworn in as the 33rd president on April 12, 1945, he told reporters, "I felt like the moon, the stars, and all the planets had fallen on me."

kinds, the largest assembly of ships in the war. The U.S. soldiers and Marines fought bitter battles on land. One veteran recalled that the 10-day battle for the important hill called Sugar Loaf was fought in a driving rain that never quit:

*I remember wondering, in an idiotic moment—no man in combat is really sane—whether the battle could be called off, or at least postponed, because of bad weather.*

The U.S. Navy fleet fought for its life against wave after aerial wave of kamikaze planes. One ship, the destroyer USS *Aaron Ward*, was attacked by 25 kamikazes. Despite heavy damage to the ship, the men on the *Aaron Ward* successfully fought off the attack. As a result, the *Aaron Ward* became known as "the ship that can't be licked."

At one point, the Japanese high command ordered the *Yamato* on a kamikaze mission of its own. But the most powerful battleship in the world never reached the American fleet. It was sunk by U.S. Navy dive-bombers and torpedoes long before it could reach Okinawa.

By July 1945, the fighting on Okinawa was over. Again, the United States had won. Next was the one battle that the Americans viewed with determination and dread: the invasion of Japan.

# THE INVASION OF JAPAN

The plan for the invasion of Japan was called Operation Downfall, and it had two parts, called Olympic and Coronet. The U.S. leaders of the invasion were General MacArthur, who would command all the ground troops, and Admiral Nimitz, who would command the navy. Operation Olympic was scheduled for November 1, 1945, and would be an invasion of the southernmost Japanese island of Kyushu. Operation Coronet, the invasion of Honshu, would begin on March 1, 1946. Everyone expected to encounter the toughest fighting yet. Some strategists predicted that the invasions would "cost over a million casualties to American forces alone." Fortunately, the invasion of Japan didn't happen. The reason was that the United States attacked Japan with a new weapon, the atomic bomb. President Truman had ordered that the atomic bomb be used in the hope that it would force the Japanese government to surrender.

On August 6, 1945, Colonel Paul W. Tibbets Jr., flying the B-29 *Enola Gay*, dropped an atomic bomb on the Japanese city of Hiroshima. Just before the bomb hit the ground, it exploded in a flash of light as bright as the sun. This was followed by an earthshaking shock. A gigantic mushroom cloud rose above the flattened city. It was estimated that 68,000 people were killed and another 57,000 were either missing or injured.

The Japanese high command did not respond to the Allies' demand that they surrender. President Truman ordered a second atomic bomb to be used. On August 9, 1945, Major Charles W. Sweeney, flying the

B-29 *Bock's Car*, dropped an atomic bomb on the city of Nagasaki. The mushroom cloud rose almost a mile (1.6 km) above the annihilated city. Approximately 74,000 people were killed, and another 75,000 were injured.

The next day, the Japanese government agreed to surrender unconditionally. World War II was over.

✛ (opposite): The use of the atomic bomb over Hiroshima caused a massive mushroom cloud that rose tens of thousands of feet above the annihilated city.

Anchored in Tokyo Bay was a huge Allied fleet. Everything was ready for the official surrender ceremony scheduled to take place on the battleship USS *Missouri* on the morning of September 2, 1945. The *Missouri* was flying the flag that had flown over the White House on December 7, 1941.

When the Japanese delegation, led by Foreign Minister Marmoru Shigemitsu, arrived at 8:55 A.M., Toshikazu Kase, one of the delegates, recalled:

*A million eyes seemed to beat on us with the million shafts of a rattling storm of arrows barbed with fire. . . . Never have I realized that the glance of glaring eyes could hurt so much. We waited . . . standing in the public gaze like penitent boys awaiting the dreaded schoolmaster.*

*MacArthur soon strode on deck and gave a short speech that concluded with the words, 'It is my earnest hope, and indeed the hope of all mankind, that from this solemn occasion a better world shall emerge out of the blood and carnage of the past—a world dedicated to the dignity of man and the fulfillment of his most cherished wish for freedom, tolerance, and justice.'*

The surrender treaties were then signed. The war was now officially over. The more demanding work of building a secure peace had already begun. In addition, there was one piece of unfinished war business, the punishment of Japanese war criminals.

✠ The signing of the surrender treaties officially ended the war.

## THE REBUILDING OF JAPAN

General MacArthur, as Supreme Commander Allied Powers (SCAP), was put in charge of the rebuilding of Japan. He used his vast authority to impose a wide range of economic and social reforms. MacArthur later wrote, "I had to be an economist, a political scientist, an engineer, a manufacturing executive, a teacher, even a theologian of sorts."

MacArthur oversaw the creation of a new Japanese constitution. Also under MacArthur, women were given the right to vote. Under MacArthur's extraordinary rule and guidance, Japan transformed many of its institutions and began the long process of rebuilding.

After the war, just as they did to Nazi leaders in Germany, the Allies put to trial top Japanese leaders who had committed war crimes. War crimes are actions that are outside the accepted rules of war.

A number of Japanese war crimes trials were conducted. In a smaller war crimes trial, for instance, Generals Homma and Yamashita were tried for their roles in the atrocities of the Bataan Death March and their barbaric treatment of Allied prisoners of war. They were both convicted and sentenced to death. The largest and most famous war crimes trial was in Tokyo. There, 25 top Japanese leaders, including former Prime Minister General Hideki Tojo, were tried. The trial lasted from May 3, 1946, until November 4, 1948. The charges included crimes against humanity, of allowing Japanese army and navy atrocities, and other breaches of laws and customs of war.

All the defendants were found guilty. Seven, including Tojo, were sentenced to death. The rest received prison terms. With the conclusion of these trials, the final chapter in the saga of World War II closed.

✛ (opposite): Inside the courtroom of the Tokyo war trial, 25 of Japan's top leaders were tried, including Hideki Tojo.

# GLOSSARY

**Allies**—The name for the nations, primarily Great Britain, the United States, the Soviet Union, and France, united against the Axis powers.

**Amphibious**—Able to operate on land and water.

**Atomic Bomb**—An explosive weapon made of either uranium or plutonium that gets its destructive power from the rapid release of nuclear energy.

**Axis**—The countries, primarily Germany, Italy, and Japan, that fought against the Allies.

**Bunker**—A defensive fortification that is a man-made hill of dirt and stone that hides and protects a cannon or machine gun and its crew.

**Campaign**—A series of major military operations designed to achieve a long-range goal.

**Capitulation**—An agreement of surrender.

**Chancellor**—The supreme elected political official, usually in Europe, similar in power and authority to the president of the United States.

**Crimes Against Humanity**—Extreme unlawful acts committed against population centers or ethnic groups.

**D-Day**—Literally "Day-Day." Originally the code name for the day on which a military offensive is to be launched. Specifically refers to June 6, 1944, the Allied invasion of Normandy, France.

**Dive-bomber**—A warplane that attacks its targets by flying toward them at a steep angle prior to the release of its explosives.

**Escort**—One or more vehicles, aircraft, or ships charged with accompanying another in order to guide or protect it.

**Garrison**—A military post or a group of troops stationed at a particular location.

**Kamikaze**—The Japanese word for "divine wind." In World War II the term described Japanese pilots trained to make suicide attacks on enemy targets, usually warships, with their warplanes.

**Medal of Honor**—The highest military decoration awarded in the United States to all branches for gallantry and bravery above and beyond the call of duty in action against the enemy.

**Nazi**—The acronym for NAtionalsoZIalist, the first word of the official title of Hitler's political party, the Nationalsozialistische Deutsche Arbeiterpartie or NSDAP (National Socialist German Worker's Party).

**Soviet Union**—From 1917–1991, the nation known officially as the Union of Soviet Socialist Republics; a nation containing 15 communist-governed republics and dominated by its largest republic, Russia.

**Theater**—The large geographical area where military operations are coordinated.

**Turkey Shoot**—Term for the competitive hunting of a game bird. In World War II, the description of the overwhelming destruction of the Japanese navy warplanes with almost no losses by the U.S. Naval Air Force during the Battle of the Philippine Sea.

**V-J Day**—"Victory in Japan Day." The day when representatives of the Japanese government signed the surrender agreement (August 15, 1945), ending the war with Japan and concluding World War II.

# INDEX